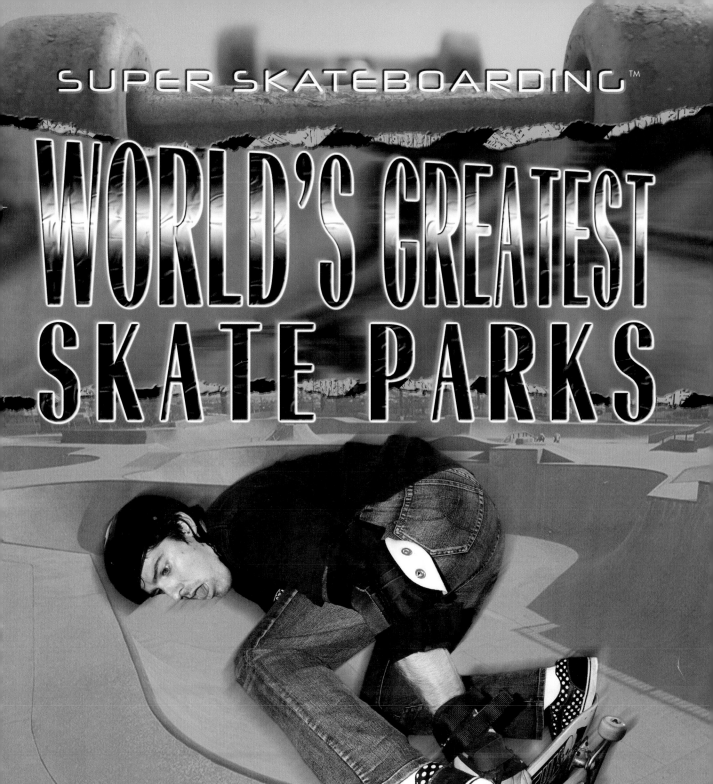

SUPER SKATEBOARDING™

WORLD'S GREATEST SKATE PARKS

rosen publishing's
rosen
central®

New York

JUSTIN HOCKING

Published in 2009 by The Rosen Publishing Group, Inc.
29 East 21st Street, New York, NY 10010

First Edition

Library of Congress Cataloging-in-Publication Data

Hocking, Justin.
The world's greatest skate parks / Justin Hocking.—1st ed.
    p. cm.—(Super skateboarding)
Includes bibliographical references and index.
ISBN-13: 978-1-4358-5046-0 (library binding : alk. paper)
ISBN-13: 978-1-4358-5390-4 (pbk)
ISBN-13: 978-1-4358-5396-6 (6 pack)
1. Skateboarding parks—United States—Juvenile literature. 2. Skateboarding parks—Juvenile literature. I. Title.
GV859.8.H636 2009
796.220973—dc22
                                                                    2008018163

Manufactured in the United States of America

On the cover: A skateboarder performs a backside air.

CONTENTS

MAR 0 9 2010

INTRODUCTION

With awesome new facilities being built every year, it's an exciting era for skate parks. This new skate park in Goodyear, Arizona, is a great example.

If you're interested in skateboarding, then you probably already know a little bit about skate parks. Maybe you've seen professional skaters like Bob Burnquist or Elissa Steamer skating them on television, in videos, and even in video games. Or, if you like to skateboard yourself, maybe you hit your local park every day after school. Either way, the chances are good you already know just how much fun these concrete and wooden wonderlands can be.

Skate parks have actually been around for a long time. The first parks were built more than thirty years ago in places like Carlsbad, California; Port Orange, Florida; and Honolulu, Hawaii. Unfortunately, as skateboarding went through several peaks and valleys of popularity, so did skate parks themselves, and most of these early masterpieces were destroyed.

Fortunately, skateboarding has reached a more steady level of popularity and acceptance in the past ten years. There are now an estimated thirteen million skateboarders in the United States, and professional skaters like Tony Hawk, Eric Koston, and Ryan Sheckler have become figures in the public spotlight.

This surge in popularity of skateboarding has also helped bring about the most exciting period of skate park construction in history. Hundreds of skate parks have been built all over the United States in the past ten years, with lots more on the way. And, as the technology and funding for these public facilities increase, a new breed of incredibly fun and functional skate parks is cropping up all over the country and the world. They're being built larger, more functional, and more fun than ever before, with some truly incredible features. If riding parks is your passion, then it's a great time to be a skateboarder.

Fortunately, skate parks aren't just limited to major cities or more populated states. Skate parks are popping up in every region of the United States: the West Coast, the Pacific Northwest, the central states, the South, and the East Coast. Each region has its own awesome and unique parks. From a legendary skate park located under a bridge in Oregon, to a 160-foot-wide (48.8 meters wide) vert ramp in California and a massive skateboard summer camp in Pennsylvania, this book is all about these insane dreamscapes—the world's best skate parks.

CHAPTER ONE

THE WEST COAST

Lots of sunshine, mild winters, and great skate terrain make the West Coast of the United States a hotbed for skateboarding. Southern California is the center of the skateboard industry and home to the largest concentration of skateboard pros anywhere in the world. Despite this fact, there has been a shortage of good skate parks in Southern California, which began with the closure of great parks like the Del Mar Skate Ranch in the late 1980s. Fortunately, the tides began to shift in the mid-1990s, and now Southern California is again home to some of the world's best skate parks.

Encinitas YMCA

Located at the Magdalena Ecke YMCA in northern San Diego, the Encinitas YMCA skate park has something for everyone. Measuring over 37,000 square feet (3,437 square meters), it's home to a large street course, several concrete bowls, and one of the world's largest vert ramps. Originally built for the 2003 X Games, the ramp is 13 feet (4 m) high with 2 feet (.6 m) of vert, and it's 160 feet (48.8 m) wide. It also has an intimidating 19-foot-high (5.8 m high) roll-in ramp, which allows skaters to drop in at lightning-fast speeds. It's an incredible ramp with some incredible locals, including Tony Hawk, Lance Mountain, Bob Burnquist, Shaun White, Lyn-Z Adams Hawkins, and Cara-Beth Burnside. The

A skater boosts a kickflip grab on the legendary Encinitas YMCA vert ramp. One of the biggest in the world, the ramp was originally built for the X Games.

Encinitas YMCA is also visited every year by thousands of young skateboarders who come to ride the huge street course and watch their favorite pros rip the vert ramp.

Channel Street Skate Park

Located in a Los Angeles–area port town called San Pedro, the Channel Street Skate Park is truly a unique spot. Since the late 1990s, skateboarders in the area had been requesting that the city government build a community skate park. By 2002, they were fed up with waiting for someone else to build a skate park. The group was headed up by veteran skater Andy Harris and inspired by "DIY," or "do it yourself," skate parks like Burnside, where local skaters took matters into their own hands and built their own park. After scouting an underused area beneath

The Tony Hawk Foundation

To pro skateboarder Tony Hawk, the legendary Del Mar Skate Ranch was like a second home during his teenage years. Having a world-class skate park to ride was part of the reason Hawk grew up to be one of the best skateboarders in the world.

Many years later, after Hawk became an incredibly successful pro skateboarder, he noticed a problem. As of the early 1990s, there were thirteen million skateboarders in the country but only a couple thousand skate parks. Skateboarders without legal and safe places to ride were being harassed and even arrested for doing what they loved.

As a response to this problem, in 2002, Hawk started the Tony Hawk Foundation, whose motto is "Supporting youth and public skate parks." By granting money, support, and advice to community groups and cities, the foundation has helped many skate parks get built. More than 365 parks, in fact, have been constructed with help from the foundation and the two million dollars in grant money it has donated. Since it hopes to get everyone involved in skateboarding, the Tony Hawk Foundation focuses on helping to get parks built in low-income areas with "at-risk" youth. A few of its success stories include the Channel Street Skate Park in San Pedro, California, and the Willamalane Skate Park in Springfield, Oregon.

the 110 freeway, they began building some small concrete obstacles. At first, it was nothing more than a quarter-pipe and some small pump bumps. Over the next year, the skate spot grew, as did the number of skaters who came to ride. With the addition of a concrete bowl in 2004, this hidden skate spot began to transform into an actual skate park.

All work was done by hand, with volunteer labor from local skaters, some as young as twelve or thirteen. The local city council eventually accepted the park and asked that the skaters form a nonprofit organization. Harris and others then formed the San Pedro Skatepark Association (SPSA). With nonprofit status, they received a grant from the Tony Hawk Foundation for five thousand dollars, which helped with material and building costs. Work continued consistently for the next several years. What was once just a couple makeshift obstacles under a bridge has transformed into a popular skate park, ridden frequently by professional skaters like Daewon Song, John Rattray, Geoff Rowley, and many others. But more important than the pros who skate there, the Channel Street Skate Park provides a great community space for a diverse group of kids from San Pedro.

Skatelab Skate Park and Museum

Located north of Los Angeles in Simi Valley, California, Skatelab is one of the most famous indoor wooden skate parks in the country. Originally designed by legendary skate park construction company Team Pain, the park has two large street course areas with tons of quarter-pipes, ledges, and rails. Connected to the street course is a wide mini-ramp, and above that is a large wooden bowl. Beyond its great skate terrain and talented locals, Skatelab has another claim to fame. It's home to the world's first and largest skateboard museum, where you can find more than two

Here is one of two indoor street courses at Skatelab Skate Park. In the background, you can see part of the Skatelab's famous skateboard museum.

thousand vintage skateboards on display, along with all sorts of cool skate memorabilia, like T-shirts, hats, and stickers. More than twenty-five thousand people visit every year to find out about the radical and colorful history of skateboarding.

Bob Burnquist's Ramp

Back in the 1980s, it was common for skaters to build large half-pipes in their backyards. Known simply as backyard ramps, they were a great place for skaters to hang out and skate (and barbeque!). But in the early 1990s, as the popularity of vertical skating declined, most backyard ramps disappeared.

Fortunately, vertical skating made a comeback in the mid-1990s, thanks mainly to professional skaters like Bob Burnquist. One of the top vert skaters in the world, Burnquist is famous for inventing and executing highly technical tricks and for doing entire runs while riding switch (which means he stands opposite of his natural stance on the board).

After purchasing a house in the dry, rolling hills east of San Diego, California, Burnquist decided to bring back the backyard ramp. He

Pictured is Bob Burnquist's enormous private vert ramp. The framework behind the half-pipe is for a complete upside-down loop ramp.

hired the company Team Pain to build the ultimate ramp—one of the biggest half-pipes ever built—complete with an "oververt," or beyond vertical, bowl section, which is similar to a wooden version of the Cradle at Lincoln City Skateboard Park. Also connected to Burnquist's half-pipe is a "loop-to-loop" ramp that allows skaters to go completely upside down. Unlike most of the skate parks in this book, Burnquist's ramp is a private facility.

Woodward West

Located in Stallion Springs, California, Woodward West is a summer camp for skateboarding and other action sports. While not quite as large as the original Camp Woodward in Woodward, Pennsylvania, Woodward West has some incredibly futuristic skate terrain. Built in 2003, Woodward West's Hangar 18 skate park is 54,000 square feet (5,017 sq m), the biggest building ever created solely for skateboarding and other action sports. Hangar 18 contains just about every kind of skateboard obstacle imaginable, from foam pits, handrails, pyramids, beginner and expert street courses, bowls, and vert ramps.

Along with Hangar 18, Woodward West has an outdoor park called the Enterprise. According to Woodward's Web site, the Enterprise's mission is to "provide one of the most progressive riding areas ever created . . . to provide never-before seen blends using wood and Skatelite, to boldly go where no skate park has gone before." Named after the spaceship *Enterprise* in the classic TV and film series *Star Trek*, this skate park looks like something from outer space, with a unique combination of bowls, half-pipes, and street obstacles, all connected in one area. In addition to this progressive skate wonderland, Woodward West also has three other skate parks: an outdoor vert ramp area, a street course called Poco Loco, and a concrete skate park called the Crater.

CHAPTER TWO

THE PACIFIC NORTHWEST

Despite rainy winters, the Pacific Northwest is home to many of the best skate parks in the world. Thanks to excellent builders like Dreamland Skateparks, Grindline Designs, and Airspeed Skateparks, there are countless world-class skate parks all up and down the coast of Oregon and Washington, as well as in inland cities like Portland, Oregon, and Hailey, Idaho. Packed with miles of green forests, rivers, and rugged coastline, the Pacific Northwest is a great place to visit. And, with legendary skate parks like Burnside and Lincoln City, it's also a great place to skate.

Burnside Skate Park

During the early 1990s, Portland skateboarders found themselves with few places to ride. Skateboarding was banned in downtown Portland, and skaters sometimes faced heavy fines just for skating down sidewalks. Headed up by legendary local skateboarders like Mark "Red" Scott, Bret Taylor, Osage Buffalo, and Sage Bolyard, the skaters of Portland began constructing their own makeshift skate park below the Burnside Bridge. With absolutely no money from the city and an all-volunteer labor force, the Burnside Skate Park began to slowly take place. What started out as a small collection of banks, quarter-pipes, and bowls soon

Located under the Burnside Bridge in Portland, Oregon, Burnside Skate Park was built entirely by skateboarders. In fact, nearly every year skaters add new elements and make improvements to this legendary skate park.

grew into what many skaters consider the best skate park in the world, a place where skaters from all over the country and the world come to ride. Burnside is home turf for pro skaters like Chet Childress, Brent Atchley, Mikey Chin, and many others. It was also featured in the best-selling *Tony Hawk's Pro Skater* video game, and Tony Hawk himself voted Burnside as one of his favorite skate parks.

Contests are rarely held at Burnside, but every Halloween, the park hosts a huge party with live bands and skaters in full costume. Halloween is a celebrated time at Burnside because it marks Burnside's original

"DIY" is a popular term that's short for "do it yourself." For many people, DIY is a way of life. The focus of DIY is to create things yourself, rather than rely on someone else to do it for you. For instance, there are many punk rock and indie bands that take a DIY approach to making music. They record and distribute their own music, create their own merchandise, and book their own tours. Beyond being a great place to skate, Burnside is a true symbol of this DIY spirit. It's proof of what can be accomplished by a small group of people through imagination, creativity, hard work, and perseverance.

beginning in October 1990. Though many new skate parks are bigger and more seamless than Burnside, it will always remain one of the most legendary parks in the world—a true mecca for skateboarding and the DIY spirit.

Newberg Skate Park

After mastering the craft of skate park construction at Burnside, skaters like Mark Scott and Sage Bolyard formed their own construction company called Dreamland Skateparks. Dreamland has constructed some of the world's best skate parks, including Newberg Skate Park, which is considered by many as one of the best parks ever built. At almost 30,000 square feet (2,787 square meters), Newberg Skate Park is one of the largest outdoor cement parks in the world. It contains an amazing variety of linked bowls, banks, hips, pump bumps, pyramids, snake runs, and ledges.

Newberg also contains some unique obstacles that you won't find anywhere else. One of these, known by many as "the spinning volcano of death," is in the shape of a volcano with transitions all around the base approximately 3.5 feet (1 m) high. On top of the volcano is a metal cylinder that actually rotates. A few brave skaters can ride up the volcano, stall on the cylinder, and actually spin around before rolling back in.

Here is the original upper section of Lincoln City Skate Park. Built by Dreamland Skateparks, it is one of the world's gnarliest skate parks.

Dreamland Skateparks

Based out of Lincoln City, Oregon, Dreamland Skateparks is considered one of the finest and most experienced concrete skate park construction companies in the world. Along with all the parks it has built up and down Oregon, it has also constructed epic skate parks in Idaho, Montana, Indiana, Arkansas, and even as far away as Rattenberg, Austria.

What makes Dreamland Skateparks so good? Dreamland builds parks using a model it calls the design/build process, meaning that it does both the design and the construction of skate parks. In other words, Dreamland controls the whole process, leaving less room for mistakes or miscommunication that could occur between regular architects and construction crews, which usually have no experience with skating or building a skate park. The design/build process ensures that actual skateboarders are involved in every stage of construction. As the parks begin to take shape, Dreamland's president, Mark Scott, constantly reevaluates the original design, making small changes based on his experienced skateboarder's intuition about what will make the most functional and fun final product.

Lincoln City

Located on the rugged, tree-lined coast of Oregon, Dreamland's Lincoln City Skate Park is another Northwest gem. Divided in two sections, the original upper section was completed in 1999 and named the Gnarliest Skate Park in America by *Thrasher* magazine.

A second section was completed in 2002, and it consists of a tight bowl complex and a small street section under a large open-air shelter, which comes in very handy in western Oregon, where it rains about half the year. This section, also called Phase II, contains one of the gnarliest features ever built—the Cradle. Imagine a gigantic, 20-foot-high (6.1 m high) cereal bowl balanced vertically on its edge, and you'll have an idea of what the Cradle's all about. The

Cradle is definitely for experts only, and it allows a few fearless skaters to go almost completely upside down on their boards.

A third section, Phase III, was completed in early 2008. This section connects Phase I and Phase II with a steep downhill snake run that empties out into a large round pool. Incredibly steep and fast, this section definitely adds to Lincoln City's gnarly reputation.

Scott Stamnes Memorial Skate Park

Scott Stamnes Memorial Skate Park on Orcas Island, Washington, was built by Grindline to commemorate legendary Pacific Northwest skateboarder Scott Stamnes. This 20,000-foot (6,096 m) island park is filled with just about every obstacle imaginable, including an actual island. That's right—at the center of this epic park you'll find something you won't see anywhere else in the world: a very large rectangular bowl with an island in the middle. This section of the park is the most challenging, with steep transitions, walls as high as 10 feet (3 m), a roll-in, and a treacherous obstacle known as the "death box."

Surrounding the island bowl is something like a concrete bobsled course, with steeply curving inverted walls. This allows skaters to roll around the perimeter of the park in continuous circles, hitting small hips, ledges, and bumps along the way. Though the Scott Stamnes Skate Park is reachable only via a two-hour ferry ride from mainland Washington, it's definitely worth the ride.

Hailey Skate Park

Measuring in at 12,500 square feet (1,161 sq m), Dreamland's Hailey Skate Park in Hailey, Idaho, covers a much smaller space than Newberg

Hailey Skate Park's sixteen-foot-high full-pipe doubles as a giant roll-in. The skater in this photo is about to blast into the skate park at an incredibly high speed.

or Lincoln City. But what it lacks in size, it makes up for in sheer gnarliness.

The park looks like one large, complex in-ground swimming pool, with a small snake run, a more street-oriented section at the top, and a gigantic 13-foot-deep (4 m) bowl at the bottom. But what you find in between those sections is what gives Hailey its originality and scariness: a 16-foot-tall (4.9 m) full-pipe, which is basically a huge concrete tube. And if that isn't scary enough, the park is designed so that you can actually roll over the top of the full-pipe. Your stomach drops as you float up the full-pipe's peak. And dropping 16 feet (4.9 m) down the back side is like the first drop on a roller coaster, shooting you into the deep bowl at speeds of up to 20 miles per hour (32.2 km/h).

CHAPTER THREE

CENTRAL UNITED STATES

T hough the majority of pro skateboarders live on the coasts, the central United States is home to millions of skateboarders. And, fortunately for these skaters, new skate parks have been popping up all across America's midsection, from the deserts of Arizona to the mountains of Colorado and great midwestern cities like Chicago.

Chandler Skate Park

The Chandler Skate Park is located in a suburb of Phoenix, Arizona. With a good mix of street obstacles and transition, Chandler Skate Park is packed with 35,000 square feet (3,252 sq m) of perfectly shaped bowls, pyramids, manual pads, ledges, rails, and banks. With so much space and so many obstacles, Chandler Skate Park has something for all skaters—beginner, intermediate, or expert. Chandler's system of bright stadium lights also allows skaters to ride at night and avoid Phoenix's scorching daytime temperatures.

Goodyear Community Skate Park

The latest addition to the Phoenix area's wealth of parks is the Goodyear Community Skate Park. Though not quite as big as Chandler Skate Park,

A skater drops in from the concrete lip at Goodyear Skate Park in Goodyear, Arizona, which has an awesome set of bowls, full-pipes, and transitions.

Goodyear has more than 30,000 square feet (2,787 sq m) of near perfection. The largest feature is a long, curving snake run, which also contains a full-pipe capsule. The expansive street course has a wide variety of rails, pyramids, ledges, and gaps. Goodyear also has a 12-foot (3.7-m) deep peanut-shaped bowl with concrete pool coping.

Many of Goodyear's locals like to skate at night. This is no surprise, with daytime Phoenix temperatures that can reach 120 degrees Fahrenheit (49 degrees Celsius). Fortunately, like the Chandler Skate Park, Goodyear has an effective stadium-lighting system that allows skaters to ride late into the night.

Edora Skate Park

Located in Fort Collins, Colorado, the Edora Skate Park covers 14,000 square feet (1,300 sq m). Though not as large as some West Coast super-parks, Edora makes up in quality what it lacks in size. The park contains a unique bowl complex, or "combi-bowl," which consists of a large egg-shaped pool, a round bowl, and a square bowl. The egg-shaped pool was designed to replicate the Eggbowl at the historic Cherry Hill Skate Park. The lip of this pool is also lined with handmade tiles, built by one of Edora's original construction workers. A long snake run winds around the outside edge of the combi-bowl, creating many interesting lines. The snake run then dumps out into a large, flowing street course with pyramids, rails, banks, ledges, and gaps. Unlike many other skate parks with separate riding areas, it's possible to hit just about every obstacle at Edora during a single run.

Rio Grande Skate Park

Located high in the rugged Rocky Mountains, the town of Aspen, Colorado, is known for its incredible wintertime snowboarding and skiing. It's a popular summertime destination, too, as many tourists come to hike, swim, ride horses—and skateboard. There's not much street skating in such a small mountain town, but you will find the outdoor cement masterpiece known as the Rio Grande Skate Park.

The Rio Grande Skate Park was voted Best Skate Park in Colorado by *Thrasher* magazine, which is no small accomplishment for a state known for its abundance of quality skate parks. What makes it so good? It was built by the respected skate park company Team Pain, which is legendary for its skills with concrete.

Here, a young skater slides the flat bar at Aspen's Rio Grande Skate Park.

PlayStation Am Jam Tour

Along with hosting a summer camp, Camp Woodward and Woodward West also organize an annual skate contest called the PlayStation Am Jam. Sponsored by PlayStation, the contest is for young skaters, aged seven to eighteen. Events are held from mid-March to May at fifteen skate parks across the United States. Individual winners receive prizes from PlayStation and a free week of training at Camp Woodward in Pennsylvania. A final event is held in August. The top winners receive five thousand dollars, PlayStation prizes, and the use of Camp Woodward facilities for the entire summer season of the following year.

The park measures 17,000 square feet (1,579 sq m). The main section consists of several small bowls connected by spines and hips. There's also a 2-foot-deep (.6 m deep) micro-pool—a tiny version of a regular pool. It's the perfect place for beginners to learn how to drop in.

There are also some more street-oriented obstacles in the park, including ledges and a flat bar for slides and grinds. For more advanced skaters, there's also a large bowl shaped like a three-leaf clover (also known as a clover bowl), with a 10-foot (3 m) deep end.

Camp Woodward

With seven huge indoor skateboard facilities and nine outdoor skate areas, all totaling well over 100,000 square feet (9,290 sq m) of skateboard terrain, Camp Woodward in Woodward, Pennsylvania, is by far the largest skateboard facility in the world. Along with Woodward West in California, Woodward also operates a skateboard camp in Lake Owen, Wisconsin, as well as a chain of public skate parks in places like Denver, Colorado, and Atlanta, Georgia.

Pictured is the massive B3 vert ramp complex at Camp Woodward in Pennsylvania. The roll-in on the far left side of the ramp is twenty-seven feet tall!

With such an amazing facility, Camp Woodward is visited every summer by pro skaters like Ryan Sheckler, Chris Cole, Sierra Fellers, and Mark Appleyard, just to name a few. They come to ride Camp Woodward's endless lines and also to help young campers hone their skate skills.

With a whopping sixteen skate areas on one large compound, Camp Woodward is too massive to describe completely. Here are a few highlights:

The Playground

Living up to its name, the Playground is an indoor park consisting of many beginner-oriented obstacles all linked together for maximum fun. One of the main features is a 4-foot-tall (1.2 m tall) mini half-pipe with extensions, a roll-in, and a spine. This mini-ramp is 68 feet (20.7 m) wide, making it one of the widest mini-ramps in the world. The Playground also contains a 3-foot-high (.9 m high) launch ramp with a foam pit landing. The foam pit provides a soft and safe landing—it's the perfect place to try new tricks, and it allows skaters to progress gradually to more difficult terrain. On top of all this, the Playground also has a hip station with four different types of hips, and a mini street area with small rails, quarter-pipes, and a bank-to-wall.

PlayStation Lounge

The Lounge is one of the oldest indoor facilities at Woodward, containing a kidney-shaped bowl, a 5.5-foot-tall (1.7 m tall) mini half-pipe, and a 4-foot-tall (1.2 m tall) bank ramp. For skaters who need a break from shredding, the PlayStation Lounge includes a video gaming area that's packed with PlayStation video game consoles, as well as a juice and smoothie bar.

The Rock

True to its name, most of Camp Woodward's skate obstacles are made from wood. In 2002, Woodward Camp owners called in Team Pain to mix things up a little. Team Pain built a 20,000-square-foot (1,858 sq m) outdoor concrete skate park featuring shallow pools, deep pools, hips, ledges, and much more. Even though it hurts more to fall on concrete than wood, the Rock is one of Camp Woodward's most popular skate parks.

B3 Vert Ramps

B3 is an outdoor complex made up of two back-to-back vert ramps. The smaller of the two ramps is 12 feet (3.7 m) high. The larger ramp is 13 feet (4 m) tall and includes a 27-foot-high (8.2 m high) roll-in ramp!

Lot 8

One of the oldest and most famous of Woodward's indoor parks, Lot 8 is made up of a giant foam pit, a 9-foot-tall (2.7 m tall) vert ramp with a 6-foot (1.8 m) extension, a 4-foot (1.2 m) mini-ramp, and a street course with several pyramids, rails, quarter-pipes, and a fun box. The foam pit in Lot 8 is much larger than the one found in the Playground, allowing advanced riders to launch well overhead and attempt tricks involving multiple spins and upside-down flips.

Wilson Beach Skate Park

Located in a public park near downtown Chicago, Illinois, this 22,000-square-foot (2,044 sq m) skate park has something for everyone. Built by the respected skate park construction company Site Design, the park contains a large street area with ledges, stairs, quarter-pipes, and handrails. A large intermediate bowl section in the center of the park contains different sized quarter-pipes, hips, and corners, along with a small L-shaped island. The expert bowl section in the back contains a large clover bowl with concrete pool coping. Chicago is home to some of the country's best street skating, but no trip to the Windy City is complete without a stop at Wilson Beach Skate Park.

CHAPTER FOUR
SOUTHERN UNITED STATES

Southern states like Florida have been skateboarding hot spots for decades. Florida is home to one of the most popular indoor skate parks, Skate Park of Tampa (also known as SPoT), and also one of the oldest existing skate parks (Kona). And one of the biggest and best skate parks in the world—the Louisville Extreme Park—is located in Kentucky.

Kona Skate Park

Located in Jacksonville, Florida, Kona Skate Park was built in the 1970s, and it is one of the only existing skate parks from that era. In its early days, Kona was ridden by famous pro skaters like Steve Caballero, Tony Hawk, Christian Hosoi, and Neil Blender. Though it has some modern additions, Kona retains some classic old-school features. Most of the older features are concrete, such as a long, flowing snake run; a kidney-shaped bowl; and a freestyle area with small concrete transitions. There's also a unique feature called the J-run. The J-run is a downhill run with a tight berm leading to a round bowl. Kona also contains a newer wooden vert ramp, a big street course, and a mini street course for beginners.

Kona was one of the skate parks featured in *Tony Hawk's Pro Skater 4*. It is also home to the Florida Bowlriders Cup, a series of four contests

This classic section of the Kona Skate Park, in Jacksonville, Florida, was built more than thirty years ago.

held throughout Florida, with the final division taking place at Kona Skate Park. The 2007 winner of the Florida Bowlriders Cup was Benji Galloway. Kona Skate Park was also included in *Thrasher* magazine's 2004 King of the Road contest, featuring pros like Jamie Thomas and Tommy Sandoval.

Skate Park of Tampa

Owned and operated by dedicated skateboarders, SPoT is one of the most well-known indoor skate parks in the country. On top of SPoT's great facilities and large crew of talented skaters, this skate park's main claim to fame is the SPoT Amateur Contest and the SPoT Pro Contest, two of skateboarding's most popular yearly events. The SPoT Amateur Contest is a proving ground for young skaters. Hundreds of amateurs travel to Tampa each year to take part in the contest. The first-place winner usually receives media coverage and sponsorship offers. Many former SPoT winners go on to be professionals, following the path of famous pro skaters like Nyjah Huston and Andrew Reynolds.

Above, a young skater pops a melon-grab over the pyramid during one of the famous SPoT Amateur Contests. The top SPoT AM winners often go on to become pro skateboarders.

The Skate Park of Tampa consists mainly of a large street course with gaps, rails, ledges, quarter-pipes, banks, and more. SPoT's street course is unique in that the owners reorganize and rebuild the street course every year, just before the annual SPoT contests. The park also includes a bowl and outdoor vert ramp. Another feature that makes SPoT unique is the Transitions Art Gallery, where skateboard-related visual art is displayed and all-ages punk rock shows are held regularly.

Louisville Extreme Park

Since its opening in 2002, the Louisville Extreme Park in Louisville, Kentucky, has become known as one of the biggest and best outdoor concrete skate parks in the world. It has a whopping 40,000 square feet (3,716 sq m)

Create a Skate

For skaters who need a break from riding, Woodward offers recreational activities like rock climbing, swimming, and horseback riding. Campers who want a more hands-on, creative challenge can also participate in the Create a Skate program. Founded by Paul Schmitt (also known as "Professor Schmitt"), this program allows skaters to actually create their own skateboard decks. Professor Schmitt owns and operates one of the largest skateboard factories in the country. Called PS Stix, the company manufactures skateboard decks for many of the world's top skateboard companies. In fact, in 2005, his company reached an incredible milestone by producing its ten millionth skateboard. Professor Schmitt created the Create a Skate program to share some of his knowledge and to give younger folks the opportunity to learn skills like mathematics, chemistry, art, and ecology, all while building something fun. Create a Skate is also available in public schools. Junior high and high school students who are interested in bringing this unique program to their school can get more information on the CreateAskate.org Web site.

of concrete skating surface, which includes an enormous, 24-foot (7.3 m) full-pipe, two 11-foot-high (3.4 m high) bowls, two 8-foot (2.4 m) bowls, two 4-foot (1.2 m) bowls, and a 6-foot (1.8 m) bowl. The street course features pyramids, fun boxes, rails, ledges, manual pads, and many more obstacles. The Louisville Extreme Park also has a 12-foot-high (3.7 m high) wooden vert ramp with a 13-foot (4 m) extension. The City of Louisville has plans to build a second phase of the skate park, which will include a 20,000-square-foot (1,858 sq m) building with indoor skate areas and concession stands.

In its first year of operation, the Louisville Extreme Park hosted the Tony Hawk Gigantic Skate Park Tour, which brought a team of top pros to skate parks around the country. Between eight thousand and ten thousand spectators turned out to watch the Louisville event.

CHAPTER FIVE

EAST COAST AND INTERNATIONAL

Though it has fewer skate parks than the West Coast, the East Coast does have some gems, such as FDR and Owl's Head. Fortunately for East Coast skateboarders, more skate parks are being built every year. As we'll see in this chapter, some of the world's best skate parks exist beyond the United States, in places that include Europe and Asia.

FDR Skate Park

Similar to the Channel Street Skate Park and Burnside Skate Park, the FDR Skate Park is a skater-built skate park located under a bridge. Located in Philadelphia, Pennsylvania, FDR Skate Park contains concrete bowls, wall rides, pump bumps, a spine, and several pyramids, as well as a mini-ramp and a vert ramp.

The park also has an over-vert pocket known as the Dome. Several features make FDR unique, including the brick coping and constantly changing graffiti murals.

FDR is also the home turf of famous pro skateboarder Bam Margera. Several contests have been held at FDR, including the Gravity Games in 2005. FDR is also one of the featured skate parks in the video game *Tony Hawk's Proving Ground* on PlayStation 2.

Here, a local blasts a frontside air out of the bowl at the famous FDR Skate Park in Philadelphia, Pennsylvania. Like Burnside, FDR was built entirely by skateboarders.

Owl's Head Skate Park

The Big Apple, otherwise known as New York City, might seem like an unlikely place for a world-class skate park. But New York has a thriving skate scene, especially after the addition of a public skate park in the borough of Brooklyn. With an amazing view of the famous skyscrapers of lower Manhattan, the Owl's Head Skate Park has both wooden obstacles and concrete bowls, including a kidney-shaped pool that was built by famous skate park designer Wally Holladay. This pool has a 9-foot (2.7 m) deep end and a 5-foot (1.5 m) shallow end, with concrete coping. Fortunately for New York's skaters and tourists, Owl's Head is located just off one of the city's main subway lines.

Skateboarding continues to grow in popularity, not just in the United States but all over the world in places like Brazil, Spain, South Africa, and Japan. And just like America, many of these countries are building cutting-edge skate parks. From a mega-park in Sweden to a monster-park in China, some of the world's best skate parks are on the other side of the globe.

As seen here, smooth concrete and clean lines make Sweden's Malmö Skate Park one of the best in all of Europe.

Malmö Skate Park

The Malmö Skate Park is located in Malmö, Sweden, just across the river from Copenhagen, Denmark. At 27,000 square feet (2,508 sq m), it's one of Europe's largest skate parks. With a creative combination of transitions, bowls, and street elements, it's also one of the world's most unique parks. Unlike many American parks, Malmö contains a wide-open street-style plaza, consisting of stairs and ledges. Connected to this area is the park's central section, which contains a large snake run with hips, pump bumps, several spines, banks, bowls, extensions, and a kidney pool. With so many different obstacles, there are endless possibilities for creative lines at Malmö. For this reason, the final event of the Quiksilver Bowlriders contest is held

each summer at Malmö. Danish skater Rune Glifberg won the Quiksilver Bowlriders contest in 2007.

Wave House

Located in Durban, South Africa, the Wave House skate park is part of a large action-sports complex. The main attraction is the D-Rex wave machine. The D-Rex simulates an actual ocean wave, allowing surfers to practice their skills. The Wave House also contains a large, 43,000-square-foot (3,995 sq m) skate park. Originally designed by Tony Hawk, the Wave House skate park has a large vert ramp, three street courses, a concrete bowl and a snake run, and a mini-half-pipe with a spine.

SMP Skate Park

With more than 147,000 square feet (13,657 sq m) of skateable surface, the SMP Skate Park in Shanghai, China, is considered to be one of the world's largest public skate parks. Containing just about every conceivable obstacle, the SMP Skate Park is made up of eleven or more sections. Here are a few highlights:

Vert Ramp

At 170 feet (52 m) wide, the SMP vert ramp is the biggest in the world. With heights ranging between 13 feet (4 m) and 17 feet (5.2 m), it's also one of the tallest.

Street Plaza Area 1

Covered by a large sun shade, this 44,000-square-foot (4,088 sq m) area contains a wide variety of banks, stairs, gaps, and ledges. Many of the

Pictured here is a large concrete bowl area in China's enormous SMP Skate Park. In the foreground are the double clover bowls and the Double Cup Bowl, with the Mondo Bowl in the background.

ledges are made from local Chinese granite. Granite is a very hard, smooth material that's perfect for grinds.

Competition Area

Set at the center of a stadium with seating for up to five thousand people, the competition area contains a 13-foot-high (4 m), 39-foot-wide (11.9 m) vert ramp. The competition area also has a large street course, with a fun box, hips, gaps, ledges, handrails, and gaps.

Double Cup Bowl

This 8-foot-deep (2.4 m) bowl has two opposing "cups," which are very similar to the Cradle at Lincoln City.

Mondo Bowl

The Mondo Bowl is a giant, horseshoe-shaped bowl with heights ranging between 10 feet (3 m) and 17 feet (5.2 m). At the center of the Mondo Bowl is a giant over-vert half-pipe that ends in an upside-down capsule-shaped bowl.

16-Stair Hubba

Modeled after the famous Hubba Hideout ledge in San Francisco, the SMP Hubba is made up of two granite ledges that descend down a flight of sixteen stairs.

Skate Parks of the Future

With massive, technically advanced skate parks like SMP in China and the Louisville Extreme Park in Kentucky, it seems like the skate parks of the future have already arrived. But with so many skilled builders pushing the limits of skate park design, the skate parks of tomorrow will only continue to get bigger and better. For instance, Dreamland Skateparks designers have plans for a two-level skate park called the Monster Park. To get from the Monster Park's top level to the bottom, skaters will be able to shoot down a super-steep spiral snake run. With so many amazing parks in existence and some insane designs on the horizon, the future definitely looks bright for skate parks.

GLOSSARY

bank A steep slope, or embankment, usually made out of concrete.

bowl A special type of skate structure that's shaped like a giant bowl. Variations of bowl shapes include clover and kidney shapes.

death box A gap at the top of a pool or bowl.

deck The flat surface at the top of a ramp or bowl where skaters wait before taking their next turn.

drop in To enter a ramp from the deck.

full-pipe A round tube, usually about 20 feet (6 m) high.

grind A trick in which you slide on your trucks on the edge of a surface, such as a ledge or a rail.

island A tall, rounded pillar with transitions all around, sometimes found in the center of a skate bowl.

ledge A short, square object used for grinds and slides.

line A series of skateboard tricks done together in a row.

manual pad A low, flat platform that is used for tricks done while balancing on the back wheels only.

pump bump An obstacle designed to help you get extra speed by pumping over transitions.

pyramid A skate obstacle that resembles the shape of a pyramid with the top cut off.

snake run A series of long, interconnected bowls that form the shape of a snake.

spine An obstacle formed when two half-pipes are connected in the middle.

transition A word for any upward-curving skating surface.

vert ramp The largest type of half-pipe, with transitions that are completely vertical at the top.

FOR MORE INFORMATION

Dreamland Skateparks
960 Southeast Highway 101, PMB 384
Lincoln City, OR 97367-2622
(503) 577-9277
Web site: http://www.dreamlandskateparks.com
Dreamland is one of the premiere skate park design companies.

Skatelab Indoor Skate Park and Museum
4226 Valley Fair Street
Simi Valley, CA 93063
(805) 578-0040
E-mail: info@skatelab.com
Web site: http://www.skatelab.com
One of the most innovative skate parks and museums, Skatelab has two locations:
     one in Simi Valley, California, and the other in Atlantic Beach, Florida.

Skate Park of Tampa
4215 East Columbus Drive
Tampa, FL 33605
(813) 621-6793
E-mail: info@skateparkoftampa.com
Web site: http://www.skateparkoftampa.com
Skate Park of Tampa, or SPoT, is one of the leading skate parks where many
     competitions are held each year.

Tony Hawk Foundation
1611-A S. Melrose Drive, #360

Vista, CA 92081
(760) 477-2479
Web site: http://www.tonyhawkfoundation.org
Launched by legendary skater Tony Hawk, this foundation helps communities
    build places for its residents to skate safely.

Woodward Camp, Inc.
P.O. Box 93, 134 Sports Camp Drive
Woodward, PA 16882
(814) 349-5633
E-mail: office@campwoodward.com
Web site: http://www.campwoodward.com
Woodward is one of the first mega skate parks, with ramp and street courses.

Web Sites

Due to the changing nature of Internet links, Rosen Publishing has
developed an online list of Web sites related to the subject of this book.
This site is updated regularly. Please use this link to access the list:

http://www.rosenlinks.com/ssk/wgsp

FOR FURTHER READING

Brooke, Michael. *The Concrete Wave: The History of Skateboarding.* Toronto, Canada: Warwick Publishing, 1999.

David, Jack. *Big Air Skateboarding.* New York, NY: Children's Press, 2007.

Heller, Rebecca. *Skater Girl: A Girl's Guide to Skateboarding.* Berkeley, CA: Ulysses Press, 2006.

Hocking, Justin. *Dream Builders: The World's Best Skate Park Creators.* New York, NY: Rosen Publishing, 2005.

Hocking, Justin. *Taking Action: How to Get Your City to Build a Public Skate Park.* New York, NY: Rosen Publishing, 2005.

McClellan, Ray. *Skateboard Vert.* New York, NY: Scholastic, 2008.

Thrasher Magazine. *Thrasher: Insane Terrain.* New York, NY: Universe Publishing, 2001.

BIBLIOGRAPHY

Brooke, Michael. *The Concrete Wave: The History of Skateboarding.*
Toronto, Canada: Warwick Publishing, 1999.

Burnside Project. "Burnside History." Retrieved March 29, 2008 (http://
burnsideproject.blogspot.com).

Cherry Hill Skate Park. "The History of Cherry Hill Skate Park."
Retrieved March 30, 2008 (http://cherryhillskatepark.com).

Concrete Disciples. "Goodyear, Arizona," "Chandler, Arizona,"
"Wilson Beach Skate Park, Illinois," "FDR Skate Park," and
"Owl's Head Skate Park." Retrieved March 11, 2008 (http://www.
concretedisciples.com).

CreateAskate.org. "About CreateAskate.org." Retrieved March 21, 2008
(http://www.createaskate.org/about_who.php).

Dreamland Skateparks. "Newberg, Oregon," "Hailey, Idaho," and
"Lincoln City, Oregon." Retrieved March 11, 2008 (http://www.
dreamlandskateparks.com).

Grindline.com. "Grindline Skate Parks: Scott Stamnes Memorial
Skatepark." Retrieved March 30, 2008 (http://grindline.com/cgi-bin/
view.pl?view=orcas).

Hocking, Justin. *Dream Builders: The World's Best Skate Park Creators.*
New York, NY: Rosen Publishing, 2005.

Hocking, Justin. *Skate Parks.* New York, NY: Rosen Publishing, 2006.

Kona Skate Park. "Kona Skate Park." Retrieved March 21, 2008 (http://
www.konaskatepark.com/kona/index.html).

LouisvilleKy.gov. "Louisville Extreme Park." Retrieved March 30, 2008
(http://www.louisvilleextremepark.org).

Magdalena Ecke Family YMCA. "Skate Park." Retrieved March 23, 2008
(http://209.200.114.27/pub/skate).

San Pedro Skatepark Association. "The History of the Channel Street Skate Park." Retrieved March 25, 2008 (http://www. sanpedroskateparkassociation.org/Channel_Street/%22 The_Story%22_2002-2008.html).

Skatelab. "Indoor Skate Park and Museum." Retrieved March 14, 2008 (http://www.skatelab.com/museum).

SkateParkofTampa.com. "Skate Park of Tampa." Retrieved March 21, 2008 (http://www.skateparkoftampa.com/spot/default.aspx).

Tony Hawk Foundation. "Kids Deserve a Place to Grow: Tony Hawk Answers the Call to Action." Retrieved March 2008 (http://www. tonyhawkfoundation.org/background.asp).

Woodward. "Camp Woodward: Our 17 Parks." Retrieved March 21, 2008 (http://www.campwoodward.com/wweast/home.html).

Woodward West. "Woodward West: Our Parks." Retrieved March 21, 2008 (http://www.campwoodward.com/wwwest/main.html).

INDEX

About the Author

Justin Hocking lives and skateboards in Portland, Oregon, where he is the executive director of the Independent Publishing Resource Center (www.iprc.org). He is the author of more than a dozen books about skateboarding.

Photo Credits

Cover (background), p. 4 (inset) courtesy www.sitedesigngroup.com; cover (right), p. 1 © www.istockphoto.com/Christian Carroll; cover (left) © www.istockphoto.com/Jenny Hill; p. 3 © www.istockphoto.com/Shane White; pp. 4–5 © www.istockphoto.com/Richardson Maneze; p. 8 © Eduardo Contreras/Zuma Press; p. 11 © Todd Huber/www.skatelab.com; p. 12 Courtesy Team Pain; p. 15 Wikipedia; p. 17 © *Thrasher* magazine; p. 20 Courtesy Dreamland Skateparks/www.dreamlandskateparks.com; p. 23 © Michael Clawson/West Valley View; p. 25 © Jordan Curet/*The Aspen Times*; pp. 27, 39 © AP Images; p. 31 © Troy Battles/Krona Skatepark; p. 32 Photo by Rob Meronek - Courtesy of Skatepark of Tampa; p. 36 © Bryan Karl Lathrop; p. 37 © Alex Farnsworth/The Image Works; background and decorative elements © www.istockphoto.com/Dave Long, © www.istockphoto.com/David Kahn, © www.istockphoto.com/Alice Scully; © www.istockphoto.com/Leif Norman, © www.istockphoto.com/Ron Bailey; © www.istockphoto.com/jc559; © www.istockphoto.com/Reid Harrington; © www.istockphoto.com/Lora Clark.

Designer: Nelson Sá; Editor: Nicholas Croce
Photo Researcher: Amy Feinberg